PORTRAIT
OF THE QUINCE
AS AN OLDER
WOMAN

Ellen Phethean

RED SQUIRREL PRESS

First published in the UK in 2014 by Red Squirrel Press
www.redsquirrelpress.com

Red Squirrel Press is distributed by Central Books
and represented by Inpress Ltd.
www.inpressbooks.co.uk

Designed and typeset by Gerry Cambridge
gerry.cambridge@btinternet.com
Set in Comenius Pro and Lithos Pro

A CIP catalogue is available from The British Library.

ISBN: 978 1 906700 90 4

Printed by Martins the Printers
www.martins-the-printers.co.uk

Contents

'…love your solitude and try to sing out with the pain it causes you.'

Rainer Maria Rilke, *Letters to a Young Poet*

for Helena, Angela, Ellen and Penny

The Bond

Tick, tick, tick, the clock tricks
minutes into the past, shadows move
across the photograph as earth turns

you along with it, lying in
bed—this is your life asleep
dreaming otherwise.

That particular ache plucking
at your ribs is an aide-memoire:

there's nowhere to travel but the future,
nowhere to live but in hours.

Get up. Get up and walk into the day.

How to Begin

Imagine every date and event
logged on a piece of paper—this is your life.
Scrunch it up, throw it in the bin.

Picture it as a video sliced in two,
you only have the first half:
it's all past tense.

Like seeing through glass,
everything you thought you knew
distorts into question marks.

Estranged, faux, sham,
memory itches like a phantom limb
you cannot scratch.

Those feelings: laughter,
vanity, self-pity, anger,
love, hurt—

score each through with a stanley knife,
create patterns on a silkscreen,
print a T-shirt.

Avoid anniversaries.
Read to escape. Write, vice versa.
Learn a skill that develops soft tissue.

Imagine a Witness Protection Programme,
being given a fresh persona.
Use that new muscle.

The Wrong House

The move was a mistake, I knew.
Sound, you said, *carries.*
We turned the garage into studios,
you hired an office, shifted desks to town.
You'd take a train or, further, jet away
to bare white rooms and music of the sea.
We boxed and coxed our bed, met at lunch or tea,
on the landing, even airports: Gatwick,
off for *family time.* There was a dream
of Spain—we searched for land, a plot, and yet
we never found the spot: too little cash,
no peace or quiet, all the drawbacks.
And love was not enough.

The Gardener

Quart bottles empty of vodka
grew among the tangle
of honesty and ivy.

The birdbath, stone heavy,
stolen, returned
a week later: random acts,

sirens and car alarms,
fights in the back lane—
hard to pick out birdsong

in a garden under siege,
too loud and rampant
for composure.

You hacked the ceanothus
bought to replace the lavender
you'd already done for,

laid a concrete path,
mowed and strimmed to keep
a way through to the studio.

Repointed the entire side wall
one summer—
I took the children to the beach.

I'll remember those nights,
after the boys were asleep,
on the bench under the stars,

a glass of Rioja, a thin roll-up.
Our silence, a kind of peace.

Soundcloud

Is it heaven, no distractions?
   A place where Roland Kirk
and Beethoven rub shoulders, space for pianists,
   lots of wind, and improvising is a breeze.

Or is it like Mole Jazz:
   dark, underground, and more records than you ever had.
   Do you discuss the new technology
   that could have freed your compositions to the world?

   Remember your big reel-to-reels?
I auctioned them on ebay (with a twinge of regret),
   though I uploaded
      the Co-optimists' tape on your birthday.

   I search for signs of you on the internet,
   trawl clips on Youtube. It's like hunting through LP covers
for one particular disc—it takes forever
   and might not exist.

Dusk Suite

The sea front at Newbiggin:
it began with a Barcarolle
that moved like waves in 6/8 time,
tried Greggs' Band with a Cuban rumba,
whirling from Italy—*Tarantella Bertorelli.*
Composing for a world
that turned miners into bakers with no dough,
you kept brass breathing.

In Norway, you fashioned *Granite*—
darker, fractured, improvised.
Began *Cargo,* via Latvia,
a parallel of decay to the West End,
left unfinished.

Aubade

You are the Milky Way
arcing over me, smile soft as moonlight

you come with your garland of stars
full of promise—

          too high, too far—
fingers search the cold blue air.

The night sky wheels on,
leaves a scent of mare.

My hands touch dew-wet roses
sun has tipped

the window lip, bed,
the empty chair.

Spring, Three Years On

I stamp the ice
off my boots:
white jigsaws in the snow-dark hall.
Mahler's 5th Adagio on the radio,
pale crocus on the freshly painted sill.
All wet, white, old
and so new.

Rooks caw
in the black branches,
fallen leaves are frozen into crust,
a dog bark echoes through icy air,
a man calls *Jake Jake!*
Above the vale,
clouds reveal blue.

The hydrangea
went stick thin,
leaves turned brown,
it looked dead.
This morning, sun
lit tiny green spears:
something held true.

The Arid Collection

'where love is like water'

i.

It's in the nature of a cactus
to be single, spiky, complex.

It lives on little: stony ground,
desert, austere spaces.

Self sufficient ribs
and flutes create shade.

It thrives on silence and solitude.
Still in the dry tick of heat,

it works in the cool of night.
A cactus does not invite touch—

it will surprise with a sudden display
of lush flowering.

ii.

A tricky art, to care
for one who likes to be alone.

In Moorbank garden
Shona kneels with tweezers

pulling out weeds,
a small but necessary attention.

A cactus needs latitude,
even in this rarified air,

or it will be overwhelmed
by the fleshy roots

—resistant to most control techniques—
of creeping wood-sorrel:

the pernicious
pink oxalis.

iii.

The succulent men come each year to Ouseburn Festival,
grey wispy hair unkempt, with specimens.
An odd assortment, they give Latin names,
advice on each variety: their way is gravel,
they like neglect—don't water through the winter.
Tenacious, hardy, no sense of hinterland,
fingers tamp earth then wipe T-shirts.
Leave them be. Plump, patient, expert
survivors, accustomed to dryness.
In subtle greens shading to blue, sculptural flesh
belies their meagre diet. Appreciate them
in decades, unlike the suburban annual.
Such circumscribed lives—no effort to live with—
make them easy to forget for months on end.

iv.

The glass airlock slides and mists,
afternoon disappears.

It's hush-hush here,
fronds drip, move a fraction

a gesture caught in the corner of your eye,
atmospheric pressure hisses,

the pond winks below your feet,
beryl in its stillness.

The plants have designs on you:
palms finger your hair,

there's hot breath in your ear,
wet smears on your back,

green hose entangles your ankle.
No-one knows where you are.

Is it feather boa, fan, the vine and stem,
or shapes between that coil a living net?

Ants eat the rot you pass over.
Something flits.

Everything waits
to be solved or saved.

Ephemera

The sun pulls up the shutters over Gateshead
still winking with sleep, bus passengers
rustle free newspapers not speaking
travel in half-dark to town
where people bearing coffee cartons
walk like Magi.

Macdonalds already has a few queueing for chips,
shops are opening their eyes, mobile phones
are throwing lines across the city, lacing it up,
commuters at the station clip in office heels,
carry no baggage.
In the one-bulb lobby, the doorman
prepares to knot his black tie.

None of us know how long we've got.
Above, the sky rouges its cheeks,
the easy jet from Alicante begins its descent,
suburbs practise silence, expecting nothing.
At the end of the allotments the 08.41 to Aberdeen
follows the golden mean.

Protestation

In diaries I seek out the dead.
They've no pity for sorrow, hate
the constant beating from my heart.
Fighting to escape,
they go to ground in photo albums.
I hunt them down, tormenting
them with questions.

They won't discuss the past, play dumb;
I dissect their secrets, rewrite history.
They're tired, they say, and want to sleep.
I set up home inside their dreams,
haunting the life they lead without me.

I cry *poetry is love's protest,*
they evaporate, whisper *desist.*

Hound

It has no feet but pointed stumps
so can't escape, it stays stock still.
One socket empty, wind blown
silver ribs, and filigree of guts:
no living flesh, this beast is gaunt
from want, like holding hurt too long.
Its jaws, stretched wide, grasp the whole
of absence, yet can't make sense of what
it lacks, caught between desire to bite
and kiss, without a tongue to lick or howl.

How to Look at Bees

Get down on your knees, lean close and lift
the black-out blind. Prepare yourself for the hive:
one body, writhing skin; your own creeps.

The moving mass can hypnotise.
To really look, blink and fix, gaze
at one particular insect, don't let go—

see how it turns in semi-circles,
shakes its sting, turns and shakes again.
Is this the dance, signaling the source?

The others seem oblivious. Choose
once more—this bee stays in place
above the waxy comb, delivering its payload.

Bees amaze: endless motion,
tightly packed, in the dark impossible space,
black and gold striped thoraxes

navigate so wings don't clash, busy
with their own mysterious destinies.
Hidden in a leafy corner,

imagine the hum of a sub-station
full of vicious currents passing to and fro.
How it brings us honeyed light.

How thoughts fly off, attention drifts:
how easily you've lost your bee—
you'll never get it back once it's gone.

Paradise 1938

A club, the West End after midnight,
chorus girls in skin-pink satin
shuffle feathers, primp and zip, bitch
and line up, face the grins
altogether in a wave, cleavage tipped,
flesh and tail bone, tuck and thrust.

A resident band plays jazz and swing
for drunken men who
get it while they can,
for heaven knows, hell
is waiting for them in the wings.
Lives will change, be shucked off

as lightly as these women dance.
Some'll be saved—by penicillin.
For others, like my mother—
skimpy costume, legs split wide
and high—the godsend is a small
white roll of cotton, a piece of string.

Listen with Mother

Are you sitting comfortably? Then I'll begin…
we're going to pretend that you've got some balls.

In BBC land, mother's lap
was idle, polka-dotted, placid,
safe beside a walnut wireless—

You don't know where I'm going to hide your balls—

tuned to Daphne, draped in pearls,
who played piano, telling lies
to dogs and tidy boys and girls.

Now close your eyes,
the music's going to show you where your balls are.

In my house, mother smelt of oils,
her overalls were stained with paint,
we'd come tumbling to her call.

Did you find your balls?

She'd spoonerise, play with words,
raise an eyebrow, flash a carrot,
sashay round the kitchen crooning:

Flat Foot Floozy with the floy floy.

Ten

The year you stopped taking baths
with the boys, Alleyn Road
was long, the end out of sight.
Number ThirtyFour: coal
in the cellar and Grandma's
hyacinth bulbs, waiting in the dark.

At the top, Father's attic,
unthinkable as the stars
and in-between, Mother,
siblings, cooking,
raised voices, tears and talk.
Lots of living room.

The tall pink Hawthorne
at the front, spiky the height
you dared yourself to climb,
scraping shins—you could choose this pain.
When you came down,
the world had changed.

Not a Tallboy

His hair was a slow moving river of ice
and his eyes were a foggy day
and his lips were wild poppies growing in corn
and his tongue was the key to an empty flat
and his head was Ulan Bator
and his shoulders were sisters who lived in different
    countries
and his arms were swans in Brockwell park
and his fingers were bar optics, all single malts,
his torso a statue on the sea bed.
His legs were rail tracks to somewhere else,
his right foot was a homing device,
the left was a gin trap.
His words were an A&E call
from the ambulance ride of his life.

Miscarriage, Half Term

An outing to the silver screen,
it takes you by surprise.
The gravid downward pull
floors you to crawl
the carpet's swirling path,
through forests made of legs.

Dizzying, this dying business,
like Snow White, not asleep
but fading. A common loss—
the bitter course, insides wanting out,
heart pumping one red apple's worth
with every beat, emptying your store.

Eyes dance with particles: blue hats,
green curtains, steely hands.
Raven voices lace around the bed,
head floats, forgets itself,
losing words.
Smile, it's easy.

Silver needles you to earth,
stops you drifting. Casket now,
your hip bones girdle a waning moon,
the forest's silent,
the mirror's blank,
screen bled white.

Outside the RVI

women in nightwear propel wheelchairs,
cradling tabs, squinting at phones,
trailing tubes and mobile drips,
feet eaten by fluffy dogs:
a cockeyed committee
ad hoc on the pavement.

Beyond the reach of warning signs,
the demi-monde light up and smoke,
make calls, meet friends, share
life al fresco, dressed for bed.
They never seem to feel the cold.
Imagine if one kept on wheeling
up the road, going home.

Welsh

Your mother hated it although it was
your native tongue, but not your first. She
despatched you to a school, better class,
English words were eaten, Taffy
taunted out. You became a polyglot
in Latin, German, French, achieved
a fluency in textuality
but not in girls or sexuality.

That took another kind of country: Love,
and music was our language. You were King
of latin rhythms, tango, salsa, jive,
your meaning found its mark beneath my skin.

I honoured your heritage at the end
and played Myfanwy at the West Road Crem.

Youngest Son Leaves Home

The house is a beach—
the tide's gone out
leaving it empty, liminal.
Littered along the strand,
pieces the sea didn't take.

The whole world is in flux:
telescopes penetrate deep space,
galaxies expand, universes multiply,
but the steady moon
pulls the sea
then lets go
as it should.

Teenager

When she suckled him, red hot coals
burned down her ducts. On fire,
she cried out and pulled away,
he pulled harder.

Jutting hips and airsucked belly,
she doesn't know how he thrives.
He sacks her cupboard,
howls at the content of the fridge,

goes hunting pig and fowl—
greasy fat and flesh.
Never sated, he snaps
at offerings, snarls malcontent.

His bed's a stinking nest
of ashy smuts and bones.
At night he disappears,
comes padding back at dawn—

where did this creature come from?
She must give him house room.
Feed him still.
He is her own.

Kirk

Skinniest in his class,
told he'd a wasting disease,
he believed he'd never grow old.
With uncertain smile, wanting to please
he'd come to tea, though he never ate.

He'd ring the doorbell on frosty nights
trying to walk home in a cotton coat.
Saucer-chested, and a violet mouth,
his dusty breath was never enough
for the darkness swallowing his life.

He kept on growing, tall and thin,
left school, fell in with drifters,
grifters, his forecast
too weighty
for any thought of escape.

See him now, on his way,
one of the walking dead.
He'll not speak, can in hand, slow eyed,
he hangs by a thread;
haunting the future, his own ghost.

Next of Kin

Once, each start of term,
I'd fill in the slip.
Every emergency covered,
numbers to be called if, god forbid,
my children fell ill or had accidents:
mother at home, waiting at the end of a line
to be pulled in.

Now as I fill in the application
I mull over the question,
google it—yes, son
is acceptable next of kin
for me.

I must let him know
and hope he hasn't broken his phone,
left it in a club, lost the charger
or changed his number.

As I swim up and down, keeping fit,
staying alive, I conjure
the circumstances: knocked off her bike,
an asthma attack, fell down stairs, god forbid,
drunk
                until I can't breathe
swallowing water at the thought of it.

How to Get Lost in Your Own City

Start in Chinatown, consider dragon lanterns
and fortune crackers, the scent of savoury plums,
dusty and sharp. Listen to old women
chatter in Chinese. You pay in pounds.

Don't hesitate at William Hill,
no-one speaks, or notices you enter
this world of multiples, perms, Yankee, Canadian,
the pall of cigarettes, the smell of men and paper.

Try Brunswick Church, hidden behind Fenwicks,
upstairs, it's locked. Dither,
think about people who've gone
until a woman says 'Can I help you?'

Finally, open a street map, look at the timetable
on a bus stop you don't recognise,
down at your map again. Hear foreign voices
offer help, volunteer directions, realise

they're local, get told 'You don't come from here'.
Feel the corners of your eyes smart.
Choose a direction. Decide to go. Do not move.
Consult your watch. Let two buses go past.

If Hadrian's Wall Regenerated

Splicing the millennium coast to coast,
stolen stones form turrets, berms and forts.
When bungalows and barns and farms collapse,
we see our world is built on Rome's foundation.

Some curse the inconvenient lack of gates
the death of north east trains, the A1s end
while others rub their hands with glee, and plan
to run a frontier smuggling operation.

In the city, the Lit and Phil erupts,
losing books into the vallum. Soon
men quicken into clans, talk of blame,
threaten guns and terrorist disruption.

Westgate Road doesn't know which side it's on
and Cowgate Morrisons's in Scotland.

Poet in Pieces on the Roscommon Road

It's not Ireland but it is.
You cycle along with one leg
and no poems. It's all going horribly wrong.
Heaney and parrot will both be there,
Kavanagh's trilby is waving you on:
Will you be coming at all? he calls.
Three cows are waiting—
The Poetry Lovers.
Arseholed, smashed,
you can't remember your name,
eyes splinter, nose drips,
face splits into jagged halves.
Your man from the *Catholic Times*
takes the picture. You have your title and first line.

Young Woman Standing at a Virginal

It is afternoon, the quiet
of the house is life
at a distance: in the street, wheels rumble,
someone calls discreetly from their door.

In the kitchen the evening stew begins to simmer,
a child playing in the next room
makes tiny noises like a bird.
A young woman stands at a virginal,

playing notes, plucked out of silence,
abrupt, not quite a tune,
alone with the rhythm
of her breathing, listening

intently for something else.
Curly hair frames her face,
a necklace gleams.
She has a dreamy look, she's heard

footsteps, or thinks she has.
She's imagining the house full of music.
With light behind, she looks into shadow.
The blue chair waits.

Solitude

is a woman's good black coat
that has a hint of mothballs under *Chanel No 5*.
Its soft wool belies its tailored shoulders,
narrow lapels, pockets thin as a tight mouth.
Its lining shrrs like a sudden flight of pigeons
from the empty square.
                                    In the pocket
is the mint imperial to suck
on the journey, to mask the scent
of cigarette, smoked behind the wall
before entering

Late Song

The Tyne is still enough for clear reflection:
September's offering an Indian Summer,
I cycle through the quiet afternoon.
Here we are again, an end of sorts,
autumn's slow fall into dark.
Yet the sun's a hand upon my back,
the river smells are real.
A curlew picks along
the low tide mark
singing its lonely tune.
Cormorants dive,
rings ripple out
to nothing.

Senescence

how skin fades
   hair thins
to pencil marks on cartridge
   features lose their threshold
face is muslin
   mouth hushed
breath comes in smoke and puffs
   too weak to carry sound
eyes gather bags of mistakes

inside this drapery is bone
   to hang the years on
cells whisper each to each
   peach turns to *pouch,*
pouch to *pucker*
until the word corrupts entirely
   and word becomes void

How to Get to Know Yourself

You are working in the dark,
crouching, your limbs cramped.
Pinpoint violet, red and black wires,
live, intertwined. Feel for the tiny clips
that grip like ants, circuit boards of silver lines, trace
    them
with your fingers. Ignore the damp
growing in your pits, the pearls slipping
your upper lip. Marvel at chips, the connections invisible
to the eye, how one thing leads to another.
Notice your breathing shallow, your heartbeat
quicken—this is your body responding to a tight spot.
Gelignite, Semtex, pliable, explosive: treat them like
    drunks,
handle them like girls. Sense the balance
between control and a feather's whisk.
Visualise success, take a breath, hover,
barely touching as you set the fuse

give yourself time, relax,
trip the switch.

Tenterhooks

What time is it? murmured
from the dark side of the bed,
the red glow consulted as if digits
were slow inklings of collusion

or consent. The hours are sleeping,
half an ear for children
waking, calling for a drink.
An ankle hooks a silky shin,

a keen knee flexes, fingers coast,
explore a hip, a hinterland,
laughter turns to sighs.
A bargain's struck as daylight rises.

Palm to palm and lips on neck,
risky angles shaping love,
they tie the knot
while the door is on the sneck.

What Maps Can't Show

the argument
beside the stile
   how she sits silent in the car
refusing a cigarette
   the heat, the sweat
trickling under his armpit
   staining his shirt
how she winds the window down
   his finger jabbing at the paper
how it flies
   when the wind takes it,
and all their words,
   deciding the outcome—
how they laugh later in bed

Now She is Home

she wakes, combs her hair
teases out tangles
the wind knotted into rope
rubs cream, smooths the map of her face
washes salt of summer from limbs
eases feet into boots
cramped as houses
drinks English tea
opens post for someone
she doesn't recognise.

The past settles back
like the wash from boats
gathering force.
Floors need sweeping
pictures long for walls
woodwork tools idle
in the shed.
She flounders in the hours
forgets how to swim
or float.

Tango Night

Tango Zapatito play
and serious couples do the moves:

a man sports trainers, slacks in beige,
clasps hand and waist of a woman in trews,

her eyes are closed, their foreheads clamp,
swaying to the hiccup beat.

When one tune ends, the partners swap:
now she's with a plumper man

who's bought his leather dancing shoes,
he slips them on and sinuously

swans on a newly polished floor.
A bone-thin Argentinian

leans her body to a male embrace,
legs entwine and slew, about

to trip, yet pick up, twist, put down
toes with metrical precision.

The bassist saws his bow, cello
and accordion sing us to

this latin heaven—dancers float,
pull and push; partnerless we sit

and wish, we wish.

Dating the Muse

He doesn't want children (tick) divorced (tick)
ignore the fact he wants a *chick*, petite
and young, you don't look your age,
chin up, you'll woo him with your poetry,
click 'like' and send a message.

Notoriously fickle, he wants heels,
and lipstick one day, beat poet black the next—
if you'd hoped for more cerebral admiration
it's tits 'n arse that tup his box.

You book a croft on Mull or Eigg—perverse
he'll want the party city Glasgow.
A swank hotel in Manchester?
He hankers for a windswept Morecambe Bay;

prefers flat white to cappuccino, spurns
real ale for brut frizzante, likes his urban
highrise yet hymns industrial decay.
He'll wrong foot you at every turn

so don't ask him to dance, he'll laugh, his verse
more terpsichorean than your swaying hips.
The right word lives on the tip of his tongue,
he'll shaft you with his wit

(that's all, his feelings are entirely metaphysical).
Check out the competition—it's not you.
Look him in the eye, make mental notes towards
a poem, don't worry what he thinks, he's glum,
treat him lightly, have some fun.

Reading 'Kissing' by Fleur Adcock with 1st Year Students

—They can see no one older than themselves

They look up at me
in the seminar room
with their knowing make-up:
mascara, foundation, blusher
thick on their young faces.
These girls, their foolish hearts,
not women, I couldn't call them women,
tossing long hair, gray light years away,
with expressions of bewilderment
yes, disgust.

They read the poem blind.
They know nothing
of the delicate make-up of sex
at sixty: the blue pills, the hrt,
the generous give and take,
of easements, adjustments,
the gratefulness of arms.
I look down at them,
bare-faced, speechless,
regretful, at myself.

Year of the Rabbit

Neck measured
for your fate
not yet ready for the dry world
you huddle there, coy and curled
floating in slick darkness, harbouring a heart

we fish for names
imagine your fragile stretch
the first moment
of gravity

Re Birth

For Arthur Darling 01.1.10

The Antipodes—as far as we can go before we're coming
      home—
all upside down, they speak a kind of English, the
      landscape
resists familiarity: ferns, volcanoes, christmas trees
that bloom in summer. Count the miles, pile up the
      noughts:
no sum can give a sense of distance
from where we've come, nor the hours it took to fly.

Fellow traveller, we have no maps, there's no going back.
Through thick skin we sense light; from a topsyturvy
world of water and hint of mother tongue
we ease our cramped bones out of the belly of transport
and see the world anew. Each journey is a coming-home,
we find a route, carrying our empty hearts like suitcases.

Card

The little boy points to the sky,
nana sings *Twinkle Twinkle*.
He looks over the wooden fence and cries: *Baa!*
Nay says the horse, *neigh*.
Baa says the cherub, pointing.
Nooo says the cow, *mooo*.
Baa the blond lad points again,
the donkey laughs *Ee haw haw*.
Baa insists the little boy, *BAA*
and the sheep reply *baa*.
Then *Baby!* he says, poking with his finger.
Yes, nana says, *Baby*,
and they have a moment's peace.

Julia Darling is Frida Kahlo

Monkey beauties, laughing,
giving permission. Death
was a way of living, Newcastle to Mexico.

Frida, artist of the heart, angling
the mirror, tearing tender flesh
inside out, raw bones through voile.

Julia, goddess, eyes on jewelled truth,
embroidering the ordinary with blood and loss.
Her last performance—

a glass carriage, two black horses plumed
with feathers; a calavera catrina
under chandeliers. Frida would have dressed

her best, with blooms in her hair;
she wanted burial by fire.
Julia chose sleep in old Jesmond.

We see you, Ladies of the Dead,
talking of difficult husbands,
wearing pink, drinking in the shade.

On the Dia de Muertos, kitchen table
an altar, we'll bring your favourite foods:
soup and bread, red wine, roll-ups,

sugar skulls and marigolds.

The Sleeping Lady

Found in the Tarxien Hypogeum of Malta

A queen, relaxed in generous sleep,
her sandy stone holds mystery.

In pleated skirt and no top,
the hill of her right hip, housing her legs

like a tortoise shell as if they might retract,
slopes down to dainty feet. She's comfy,

resting there on curved divan,
right hand palming her head

and perhaps an axe,
eyes closed, serene.

Her left hand fingers an ample muscle:
she's the weightlifter's build

of a gossip with folded arms at the shops.
We might imagine someone reading to her,

or maybe she's catching forty winks,
half-listening to the radio.

She's been napping for thousands of years;
sleep is her function, she shows us the meaning of *still*.

No faceless Venus billowing belly and breasts,
fertility's not her story, but fulsome ease.

She knows how to let go, illustrates my mother's advice:
never stand when you can sit, never sit when you can lie

and reminds me of you,
never more content than when dead to the world.

Portrait of the Quince as an Older Woman

It waits in the basket, insouciant,
round of limb and buttock,
furry as a doe's back. Lay hold
and feel its heft and mass, how

it's bony as a skull. Wash it
and the down rubs off, scrub roughly till
the skin's alive and sheens with promise.
Choose the sharpest knife to reveal the core,

its coarse dry flesh will roll from the blade,
and resist unless the touch is firm. Persist, it must
be sliced, cut into pieces, for only then
will the body relent to open, soften.

Simmer in red wine or water,
with sugar and pips to help it set,
this tough fruit will burnish to a jellied rose,
with honey kiss. It takes new form.

The recipe's too onerous for those
whose appetites are raised on pluck and eat.
Aphrodite's food of love,
whose art is being lost.

Wise women know: give her time,
she'll gift her ruby harvest.
Praise the quince.

Acknowledgements

'Hound'
Gift: chapbook for Seamus Heaney NCLA 2009

'Poet in Pieces on the Roscommon Road'
'Re Birth'
The North, Issue 48, 2011

'How to get Lost in Your Own City'
Rain Dog, Issue 13, 2007

'How to Get to Know Yourself'
2nd prize, the Jitegemee Competition 2010

'Spring, Three Years On'
How Things Are Made: Poems for Gordon Hodgeon
Square One Books 2009

'Late Song'
3rd Prize, Inpress Indian Summer Comp, 2012

'How to Look at Bees'
3rd Prize Vorse Scribbin, Basil Bunting Competition, 2013

'Listen With Mother'
Double Bill, Red Squirrel Press, 2014

With thanks to

Sheila Wakefield for her support and commitment
Anna Woodford for her generous help and advice
Leni Dipple for her hospitality at Le Bourmier
Carte Blanche
The Bridge Poetry Group
The Women's Poetry Group
Northern Poetry Workshop

041304813